MEMPHIS

Translated from the French by Harriet Mason

First published in Great Britain in 1998
by Thames and Hudson Ltd, London

Copyright © 1998 Éditions Assouline, Paris

British Library Cataloguing-in-Publication Data
A catalogue record for this book is available from the British Library

ISBN 0-500-01900-2

Printed and bound in Italy

745.4

LUTON SIXTH FORM COLLEGE

BRADGERS HILL ROAD
LUTON BEDS
LU2 7EW

Return on or before the last date stamped below.

1 5 MAY 2001

2 8 MAY 2002

1 6 JUN 2005

0 5 SEP 2005

- 3 OCT 2005

2 1 MAY 2008

- 5 DEC 2008

N

MEMPHIS

Brigitte Fitoussi

Thames and Hudson

'Artists must show how to find originality,
the unexpected and independence.'
ETTORE SOTTSASS

a burst of bright colours, unusual combinations of shapes
and materials; incongruous mixtures of laminated plastic,
glass, marble, granite, metal or lacquered wood; furniture
made to look like sculpture, and as expressive as characters in
cartoon strips; stacks of shelves like totem poles, imaginary little
monuments; chairs with legs askew, tables with either two or three
ball- or cylinder-shaped legs – all with evocative names such as
Brazil, Santa-Fe, Oceanic, Diva, Carlton, Eastern. In the space of
less than ten years, the work of Memphis, the famous Milanese
design group, managed to sidestep all the rules of functionalism and
modern 'good taste'. Challenging, original and inventive, Memphis
made a lasting impact on the style of the eighties.

Memphis was set up in Milan in 1981, bringing together a group
of young designers, architects and graphic designers, from various
countries and backgrounds, around the central figure of the
well-known Italian designer Ettore Sottsass. Their unusual, even
iconoclastic work was set to turn the design world upside down, and
its impact is still important today. Memphis was enormously
successful from their very first show, and their fame quickly spread
well beyond Italy. And yet, there was no formal theory behind their

work, nor any wish to lay down rules for a new movement or a new style. Memphis took up the challenge of colour and decoration, and aimed to bring them back into domestic settings, using both expensive and cheap materials and varied styles and cultural sources.

Sottsass explained that, 'using materials and colour together produces a certain effect. It allows for greater sophistication and originality. In our work for Memphis, we had the idea of using laminated plastic to make showy and luxurious furniture, although it is normally used in kitchens and bathrooms and regarded as an essentially commonplace material. If I put a crudely coloured piece of laminated plastic next to a fragment of a tree root, an object with a certain dignity, a vibration is set up between them.'[1]

Wanting to challenge the standardization and over-rationalism of modern design, Memphis offered a new range of widely available furniture and artefacts, within a framework which was instinctive rather than functional, artistic rather than commercial. None of the members of the group had any idea of how quickly they would provoke the excitement that followed: it amounted to a revolution, and Memphis very quickly became recognized all over the world as the key to new means of expression. There was a widespread mood of euphoria, and a new generation of designers immediately welcomed the way that Memphis appealed to the imagination, and their responsive and personalized approach to industrial production.

Ettore Sottsass, the Moving Spirit of Memphis

The importance of Ettore Sottsass' role in Memphis cannot be underestimated. He was the leader of the group and the inspiration behind Memphis. A masterful interpreter of form, he conveyed an enormous, infectious vitality, although he was already in his sixties. Through him, young designers were able to articulate new possibilities in design.

A man of great charm, Sottsass is tall, with a white moustache and long wispy hair, and has a permanent expression of surprise. He loves women, football and spaghetti: he is an epicure. He is one of those people who can start a fashion or launch a style and arouse instant enthusiasm for it everywhere; except, perhaps, among the ranks of the more 'serious' rationalist architects. In spite of a certain fascination for his work and its roots in intuition and the accidental, they have often made him the subject of critical polemic: too gestural, too ephemeral, too tied up with fashion.

Sottsass was born in 1917 in Innsbruck in Austria. An architect, he became a superstar among Italian designers, and has been one of the most influential figures in the history of post-war Italian design. The route he has taken has always been very personal, but for the last fifty years he has consistently been a central player in Italy's most important cultural developments. His searching mind found inspiration on his journeys to the East in the early sixties. Among the many places he visited were India, Burma, Thailand and Nepal, where he learned about the dignity of Oriental cultures, acquiring an abiding fascination for their traditional handicrafts, their textures, dyes and techniques and the treasures to be found in their vernacular art. Here he also discovered a passion for ceramics, which were thereafter a dominant part of his own work. Soon after the Orient, he was introduced to the United States via Pop Art and the ideas of the writers of the Beat Generation. These new Western images became fused with Eastern ones in his imagination and his work.

Uncompromising in temperament, Sottsass has been a 'guru' for the avant-garde since 1947, always in the forefront of both industrial projects and experimental design. Since 1958, he has been one of Olivetti's most important designers. While in charge of their Computer Design section, he devised the majority of their new design projects – among his most well known, the first Italian computer Elea 9003 (1959), the little red typewriter Valentine (1969) and the electric typewriter Praxis 48 (1964). At the same time, he made a series of furniture designs – influenced by his discovery of American Pop Art – for the Italian manufacturer Poltronova, the most avant-garde manufacturer at the time. In 1966 he designed a witty collection of striped cupboards in screen-printed laminated plastic – the starting-point for his extensive work on colour, surface finishes and decoration, and the basis for the more extreme furniture he made for Memphis fifteen years later.

Sottsass has always been 'a counter-culture intellectual'. Looked at as a whole, his work is like an enormous collage: made of elements from daily life and based on any number of fragmentary images of his travels, and distant cultures, his furniture, his artefacts and interior spaces. His approach is almost child-like and is the result of endless investigation and a high degree of artistic sensibility. He has said that, 'Design does not mean giving a shape to fairly trivial products, for a fairly unsophisticated industry. It is a way of seeing life, politics, eroticism, food and even design itself.'[2]

Radical Design and Memphis' beginnings

Memphis would never have existed without Sottsass, but its history is equally tied up with the anti-establishment activities of Radical Design, in which Sottsass was one of the principal players. The end of the sixties was an era of protest – after American Pop Art, the beat and hippie cultures attempted to open people's eyes to the consumer society, and sound its death knell. The corrupting effect of the industrial world, the idea of standardization as a universal aspiration and vehicle of social progress, the orthodoxy and reasoning of the 'Modern Movement' (developed in the thirties under the influence of the Bauhaus and the architect Le Corbusier) all needed to be reappraised. Soon after, the first petrol crises struck, leading to serious doubt that unlimited commercial production was possible. In the sphere of design and architecture, this sparked off critical debate and philosophical reflections: projects with a theoretical and cultural purpose took precedence over functional ones. Architecture and design were now regarded as political tools, and became part of an exploration of the subversive aspects of Pop culture. In one country after another, the first signs of postmodernism and neomodernism could be seen. The American architect Robert Venturi wrote in 1966 in *Complexity and Contradiction in Architecture*, 'I like things which are hybrids rather than "pure", the result of compromise rather than one person's work, convoluted rather than clearly articulated, as perverse as they are impersonal, as boring as they are interesting, conventional rather than "original", all-embracing rather than exclusive, superfluous rather than simple, as old as they are innovative, contradictory and equivocal rather than clear and unambiguous. From what I have seen of unity, I prefer life to be haphazard.'

Around this time, two groups of architects were formed in Florence – Archizoom and Superstudio – and a few years later, in 1973, they joined forces to unite the avant-garde of radical Italian architecture, forming a school of 'counter design' known as Global Tools. They attracted both professionals, Sottsass among them, and students, and together dreamed up wild schemes for towns and housing, outrageous realizations of their political and social visions. The desire for a cultural role was behind a very broad spectrum of artistic and experimental schemes. All the members of this school were dedicated to the break up of a system which from the beginning of the century onwards had offered no possibility of self-expression beyond the limits of the rational. This did not mean that the protagonists of Radical Design wanted to become artists or craftsmen, but that they no longer accepted the rules laid down by their sponsors, institutions, promoters, producers or manufacturers. Hungry for new areas governing freedom of action and speech, they spent three years, oblivious of all practical realities, designing a mass of ironical and utopian projects.

Before Memphis, Alchimia

Tiring of the political discussions that had taken him away from his drawing-board, Sottsass left Global Tools towards the end of the seventies to pursue his own work. With some ex-Radical Design colleagues, such as Andrea Branzi, a leading theoretician of Italian design, and Michele De Lucchi, a brilliant young Florentine architect, he joined the Alchimia practice in Milan in 1977. This was a new group which had been formed a year earlier by the avant-garde architects Alessandro Mendini and Alessandro Guerriero. Alchimia's central concerns were 'the ordinary object', the 'redesigning' of everyday pieces of furniture, and the revival of past avant-garde themes from earlier in the century, from futurism to the Bauhaus. Their projects had no particular style, but mixed elements of kitsch, modern and downmarket design with a preference for decorated surfaces and high-quality workmanship. In an attempt to reassert the symbolic function of objects, Alchimia rejected the idea of mass production – they were much more concerned with mounting art exhibitions or promoting the cultural aspect of their work than with facing the real market. Sottsass had higher ideals, and was not satisfied for long with 'redesigning' and revivals; in 1980 he and Michele De Lucchi left the group, and a few months later set up Memphis.

How Memphis began

'Oh, mama, can this really be the end
To be stuck inside of Mobile
With the Memphis blues again
And here I sit so patiently
Waiting to find out what price
You have to pay to get out of
Going through all these things twice...'
(The Memphis Blues Again, Bob Dylan)

On 11 December 1980, a long winter evening, Memphis was born at Sottsass' home in Milan. In his little sitting room, over some good Italian white wine and with a Bob Dylan record playing in the background, Sottsass was going back to first principles in a discussion with a few young designers who worked in his office: Marco Zanini, Aldo Cibic, Matteo Thun, Michele De Lucchi and Martine Bedin. Although they were not there that evening, Nathalie Du Pasquier and George James Sowden joined the group shortly afterwards. They were all between twenty and thirty years old. Sottsass' partner Barbara Radice (the future artistic director of Memphis) and an old cabinet-maker friend, Renzo Brugola (who became Memphis' manufacturer) were also present. The group had been brought together because Sottsass had been commissioned a few days earlier to create an entirely new collection of furniture for Brunella and Mario Godani, owners of a prestigious showroom in Milan. The

Godanis had already shown some furniture designed by Sottsass for the Poltronova company (which had been made by Renzo Brugola). Although he no longer worked for Poltronova, the Godanis wanted to continue their partnership with the famous designer. Sottsass accepted their very attractive proposal, but suggested undertaking it as a collective project.

The group were agreed that there would be no place in their venture for pale suede sofas, chrome and smoked Plexiglass tables, walls with multiple-shelf units and beige-coloured carpets – in short, all the trappings of seventies 'good design'. As the night wore on at Sottsass' house, no one thought of changing the Dylan record which was endlessly repeating the words of the song 'Stuck inside of Mobile with the Memphis blues again'. Suddenly the name Memphis struck a chord, like a prophetic evocation of contrasting mythic worlds, meeting by chance: 'The blues, Tennessee, rock'n'roll, the American suburbs, the capital of the Egyptian pharoahs and the sacred city of the god Ptah'[3] – the patron of craftsmen.

Memphis was born. But this was only the beginning, although they had already planned an exhibition for the autumn of 1981. For several months, the members of the group met every Monday evening in the trattoria opposite Sottsass' home to compare ideas and designs. In the relaxed atmosphere, enjoying a glass of wine, great schemes were hatched. In February 1981, over a hundred multi-coloured drawings showed that Memphis' 'new design' had become a real proposition. The sketches with their zany decorations and asymmetrical shapes were made without any intention of stylistic unity, and overflowed with character, which up to now had been lacking in many 'inanimate' objects.

Everything had to be organized – they had to find sponsors, manufacturers and skilled workers, to persuade the firm Abet Print to manufacture new laminated plastics with printed motifs, to contact other designers abroad, to produce a graphics house-style, to put together a catalogue and make posters and invitations. In June, Sottsass finally succeeded in finding five people willing to form a company. One of them was Ernesto Gismondi, managing director of Artemide (the leading lighting company in Italy), who was a close friend of Sottsass and had already approached him to produce the Memphis lamps. He was so impressed by the originality of the designs that he undertook Memphis' commercial production and distribution on the international market. Gismondi became the principal shareholder. He was joined by Fausto Celati, another industrialist, Renzo Brugola, the cabinet-maker, and Brunella and Mario Godani, owners of the showroom *Arc 74*.

The big day was on 18 September 1981 – Memphis made its first public appearance with various previews, independent of the Milan Salon furniture show. Two and a half thousand people rushed to see it, intrigued by the stylized head of a Tyrannosaurus printed on the invitation. Journalists and fellow designers from all over the world were dumbfounded by this deluge of startling colours and shapes. The fifty-five exhibits – thirty pieces of furniture, three clocks, eleven lamps and eleven ceramic pieces – caused a storm. Success was instantaneous – there was a stream of reviews and everyone was talking about it. Memphis very quickly became a fashion and a cult.

Ideal conditions

Memphis was the result of the design genius of Sottsass and the boldness of the industrialist Gismondi, without whom the whole project would never have been realized. The circumstances in Italy were ideal for such a project. Most of the industries and factories connected with furniture making are located in the province of Brianza, around Milan, and offer designers great scope for experimentation. Italian design is particularly concerned with the applied arts and has a vitality because of the high level of practical expertise. In both small and medium size businesses, high technology and craftsmanship often go together, linking traditional and modern techniques. The Memphis project was also a hybrid, and made good use of this tried and tested method of production. However, although the idea was to produce and distribute furniture and artefacts using the existing industrial system, the practical difficulties were not taken into account at the design stage. This nevertheless led to an incredible level of output in the creative field during the eighties. Milan opened its arms to the world, and became the design capital, the Mecca of the avant-garde. There was a tremendous outburst in design – in fashion, furniture, graphic design and shop design. The key to the Italian way of life was the everyday consumer object and no longer a narrow idea of aristocratic or provincial luxury.

Memphis and 'Nuovo Design'

Memphis and Alchimia were jointly responsible for the emergence of what became known as 'Nuovo Design'. With a literal rather than aesthetic point of view, it opened up the way for verbal statements: a piece of furniture became the equivalent of a word or sentence, a literary or poetic quotation. It was radically innovative. Aside from their practical purpose, objects became repositories of memory, emotions and personal and collective feelings. New means of expression, centring on signs and communication, underlined a strong desire to bring domestic objects out of obscurity – by linking art and poetry with manufacturing. There was something of a revival of the spirit of the pioneering movements of the last century, such as the Arts and Crafts Movement in England, or at the beginning of this century, the Werkbund in Germany, which, in reaction against the mechanization of the Industrial Revolution, was already claiming to make 'artistic industrial products'. Sottsass' work and his guidance of Memphis certainly led to the rediscovery of the beauty of 'primitive' objects, and through them the idea of spirituality, of ritual and the importance of a particular approach to craftsmanship.

Influences

Memphis' moment was brief, and the group was very quickly trapped by fashion; paradoxically, its products were to be found in museums and in private collections before they had arrived in the furniture stores – they were bought by the elite when they were intended for the mass market. But in spite of all these contradictions, Memphis enabled design to be released from its strictly utilitarian role, and enabled designers to claim the more liberated status of artist. They almost assumed 'rock star' status, taking on new lifestyles and house styles, claiming new areas of exploration. There was the satisfaction of having the freedom to create at will, and impermanence, decoration, humour and cultural cross-breeding were all able to contribute to a redefinition of creativity itself. But after a storm, landscapes look very different. A new wave of minimalism came at the beginning of the nineties, in complete contrast with the extroversions of Memphis. All the same, apart from the styles and concepts, the idea that design had earned the right to be regarded as a powerful means of communication is now firmly established. Many manufacturers have drawn lessons from the Memphis phenomenon, and have re-evaluated various aspects of the politics of their image and products.

Contradictions

Memphis is in a category of its own in the history of design. Its creators had never wanted to produce limited and numbered editions of their work, and yet much of it is only to be found in private collections and museums. Indeed, from the very beginning, an instant market was created alongside the commercial distribution: Memphis' products were sold simultaneously in furniture showrooms and in up-market art galleries, sowing confusion in the minds of buyers. Some of the first pieces, which were still in production, were sold at Christie's in London in 1989 at incredibly high prices, although they could have been ordered at their normal price by a simple phone call to the head office in Milan. A practical object and/or a work of art, or something between the two – this is the great contradiction of Memphis, but it is also where its originality lies.

After Memphis

Although their most recent collection had been enriched by the inclusion of pieces by new, talented Milanese designers, the members of Memphis, aware of the limits of their project and the impossibility of maintaining the element of surprise that it had at the beginning, decided to go their separate ways in 1988: it was the end of their venture. All of them went on to work independently.

Today, Memphis no longer exists as a creative entity, but a company with the same name, Memphis Srl (or plc) is still in business. Alberto Bianchi Albrici, currently the managing director, is continuing the workshop production of the three hundred pieces made for the eight 'Memphis Milano' collections between 1981 and 1988, which were shown every year at the same time as the Milan Salon furniture show.

In 1989 and 1991, twenty internationally known artists, among them Sandro Chia, Joseph Kosuth, Michelangelo Pistoletto and Sol de Witt, showed a collection of furniture-sculptures, with the title 'Meta-Memphis'. These two series had no connection with the furniture of Memphis Milano, but were added to the company's range, as were subsequent collections: 'Memphis Extra' (1992, 1993 and 1994) and 'Easy Home by Alessandro Mendini' (1995).

At that time, Memphis Srl was still owned by Ernesto Gismondi, the head of Artemide, but he appointed Alberto Bianchi Albrici to be his managing director. In 1996 Albrici bought the company, determined to develop new design projects and in 1997 he opened a new gallery in Milan called *Post-Design*, where he displays and sells Memphis Srl goods and also shows new work.

Ten years after Sottsass' group dispersed, the production of the Memphis Milano classic collections is still thriving. Although the furniture and other objects – lamps, ceramics, clocks, silver, fabrics and glassware – no longer look like prototypes, they are still individually made by craftsmen.

A different landscape

Now aged eighty, Sottsass is still young and adventurous in spirit. Without looking back to the days of Memphis, he has recently accepted a commission to design some new furniture for the *Post-Design* gallery.

He explains that, 'There is no after-Memphis, there is only evolution. Memphis was not a stylistic operation, even though many people believed it was. When a new language is created, a great new energy is suddenly released; but those new possibilities need not be locked in the past. We never claimed that we wanted to "change the world". Memphis was a story of meetings of energy. Inevitably, each time we got a little further removed from the idea of design that was at the disposal of industry. It was as if we had opened a different window and said: "Look out there, there is a new landscape, if you want to you can take a walk there."'[4]

[1] *Ettore Sottsass*, Editions du Centre Georges Pompidou, Paris, 1994

[2] Fitoussi, Brigitte, 'Memphis est mort, vive Memphis', interview with Ettore Sottsass in *L'Architecture d'aujourd'hui*, no. 240, September 1985

[3] Radice, Barbara, *Memphis*, Gruppo Editoriale Electa, Milan, 1984

[4] Fitoussi, Brigitte, 'Ettore Sottsass, cinquante ans de dessins et de curiosité', in *L'Architecture d'aujourd'hui*, no. 292, April 1994

MEMPHIS

Shiro Kuramata
Hans Hollein
Emilie van Hees
Martine Bedin
Mario Godani
Andrea Branzi
Luciano Paccagnella
Aldo Cibic
Terry Jones
Renzo Brugola
Ernesto Gismondi
Barbara Radice
Masanori Umeda
Nathalie du Pasquier
Javier Mariscal
Rainbow
Luigi Serafini
Marco Zanini
Studio Alchymia
Fausto Celati
Lorenz
Ettore Sottsass
Alessandro Mendini
John van Hamersveld
Suzanne Phelps
Peter Shire
Paola Navone
Abet Print
Matteo Thun
Peter Ogilvie
Arata Isozaki
George Sowden
Michael Graves
Brunella Godani
Guido Jannon
Michele De Lucchi
Brionvega

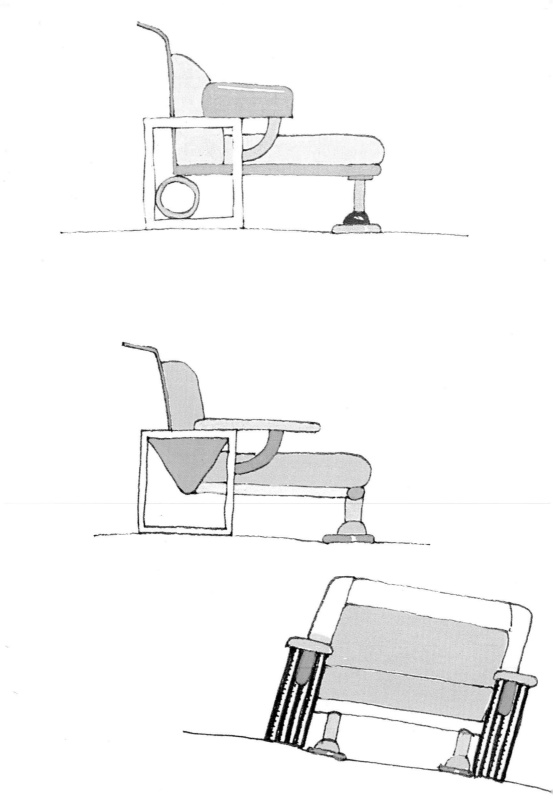

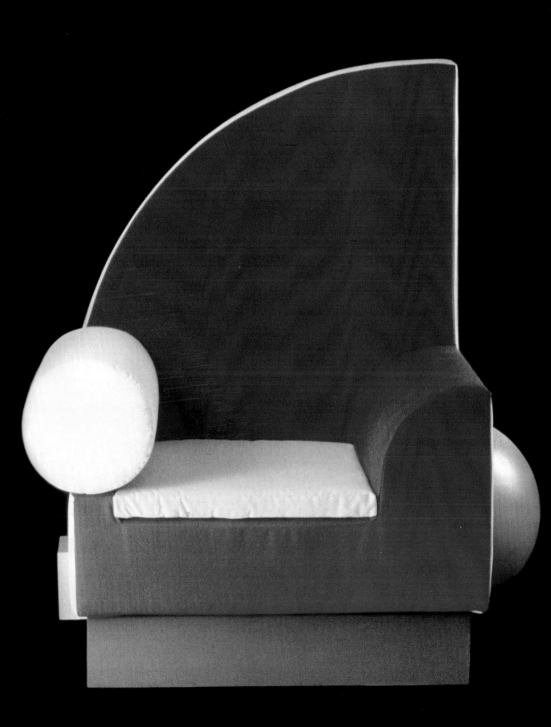

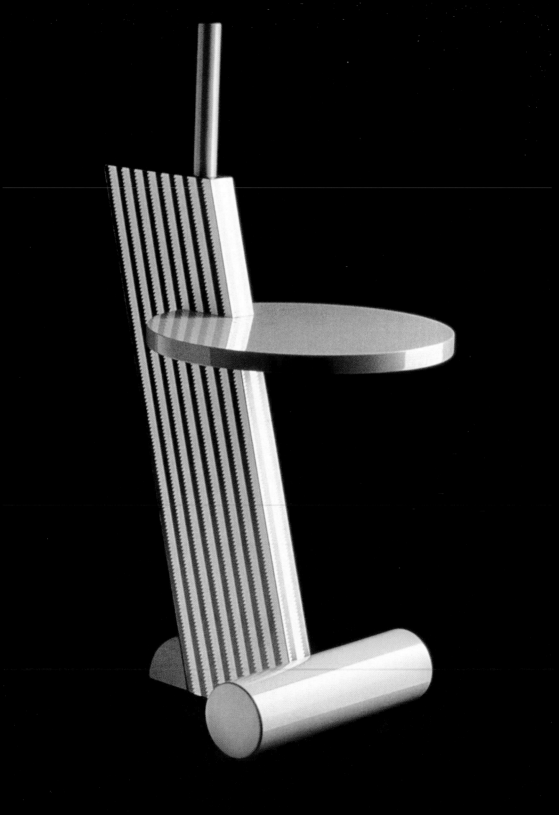

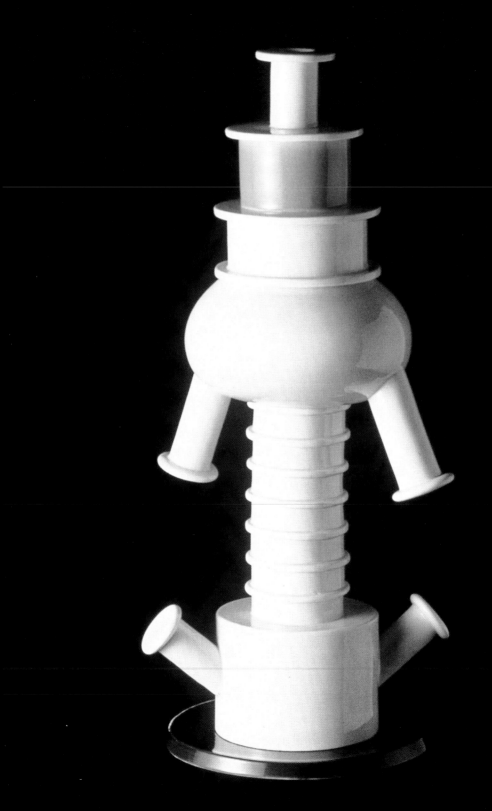

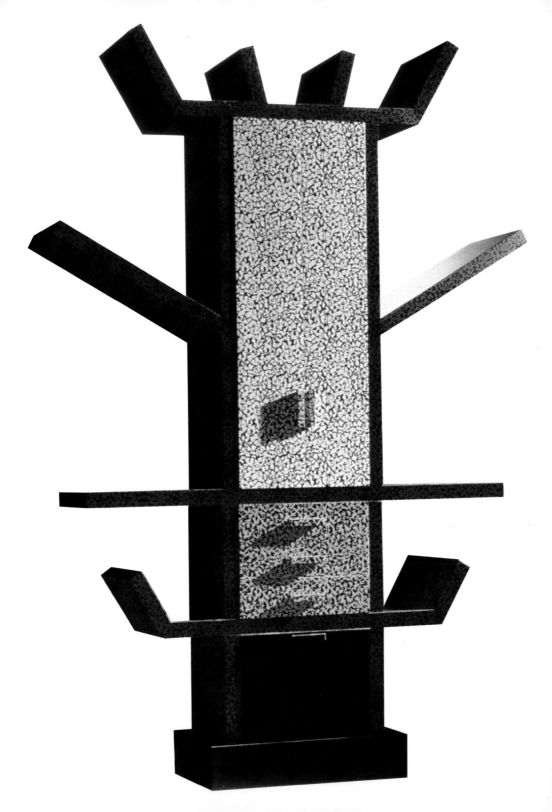

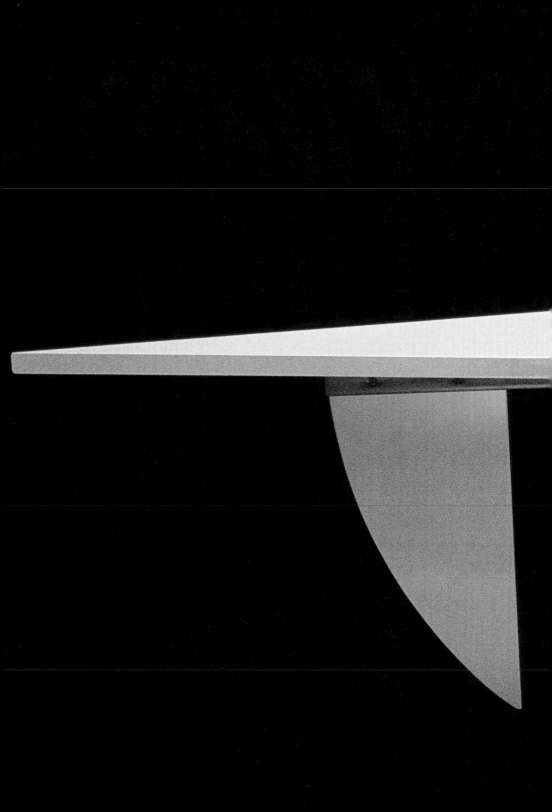

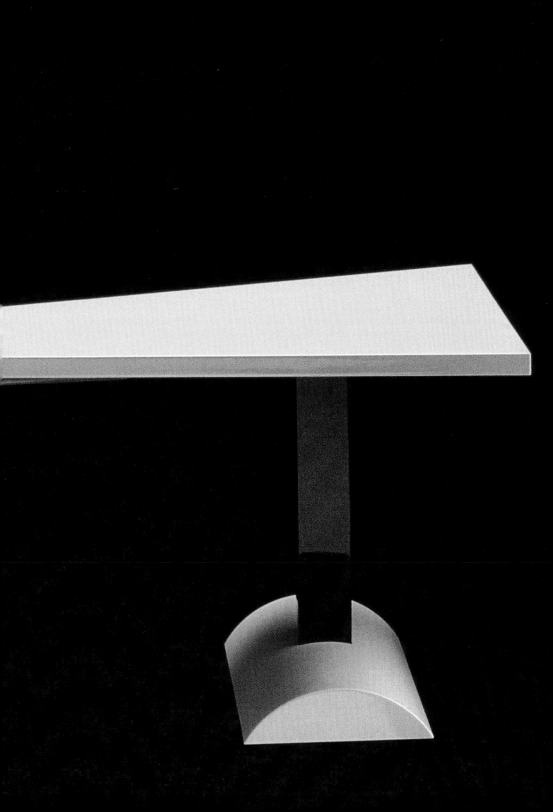

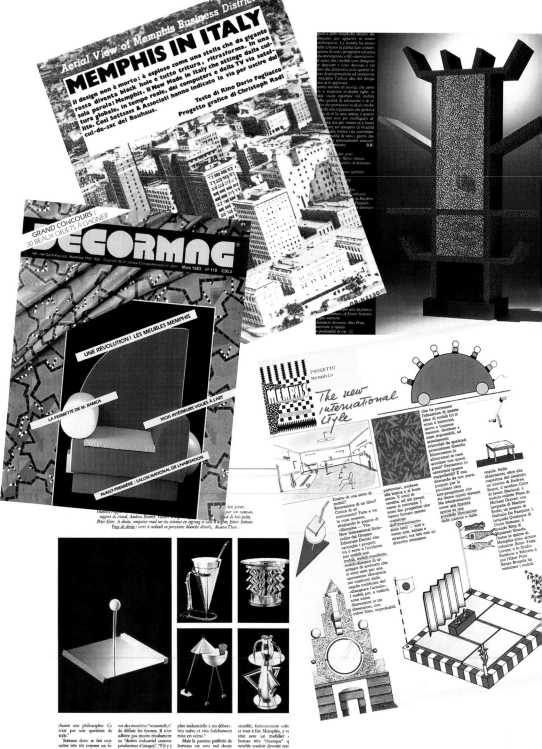

I MUTANTI

Memphis furniture:
a Milano una internazionale del design di ricerca
e le sue insopitabili creature

a cura di Barbara Radice

At Home

Part III

MEMPHIS/MILANO

New York Debut of A Once and Future Trend

By Sharon Lee Ryder

North Shore Tudor Goes Modern

4-5

modo in _____
sono fatti portavo _____
Materiali "high-tech" come _____
esasperate, non sempre rigorosamente _____
gruppo è Ettore Sottsass, architetto e designer _____
definisce il design "Memphis" "un design sensoriale: una tras _____
sensazioni più che di funzioni". Questi oggetti sono il risultato di anni di _____
ricerca e di dibattiti: elementi in cui coesistono condizioni culturali precise _____
legate alle condizioni ambientali delle grandi metropoli. Il nome "Memphis" è stato scelto in omaggio alla patria del rock nel Tennessee; alla
mitica città egiziana la cui divinità proteggeva le arti; e alla famosissima
canzone di Bob Dylan.

"Freemont" è il nome di questa credenza-libreria di Ettore Sottsass.

cronaca Milano

La Repubblica
giovedì 16 aprile 1987

Gli arredi di Sottsass e allievi sono oggetti

Memphis la provocazione ora diventa collezionismo

Da boutique di cervelli a business

di MIRIAM DASTOL

Due anni fa il salto
ma i grandi del gruppo
rifiutano di trasformarsi
in una "griffe": Dicono:
"Non ci interessa,
se lo dovessimo finire
per noi sarà finita"

La terza generazione

E il fumetto si arruola sotto le sue bandiere

Una libreria di Andrea Branzi, "Magnolia": collezione "Memphis" 1985

Uno strano tavolo a intarsi "Sophia" è stato disegnato da Aldo Cibic.

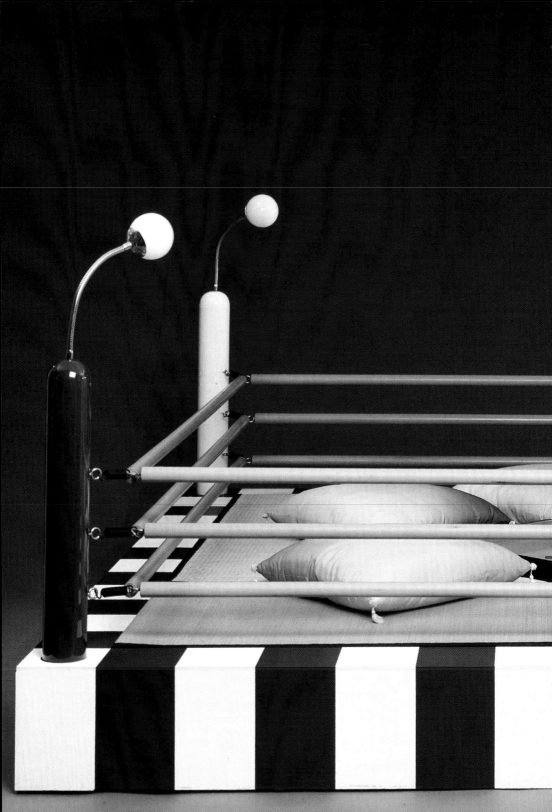

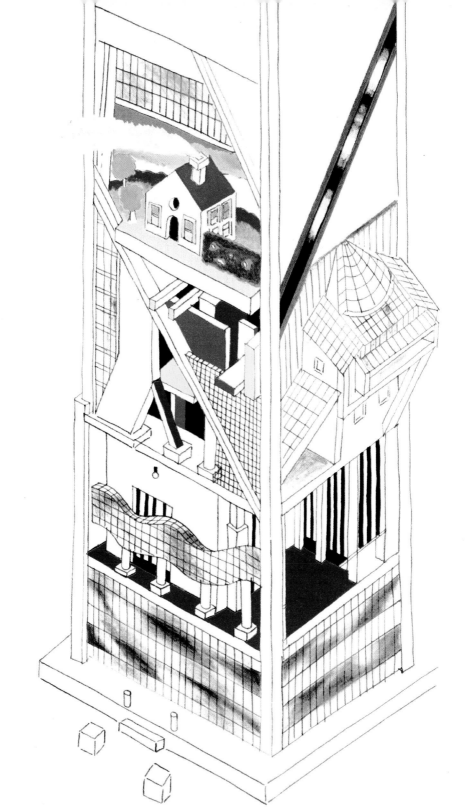

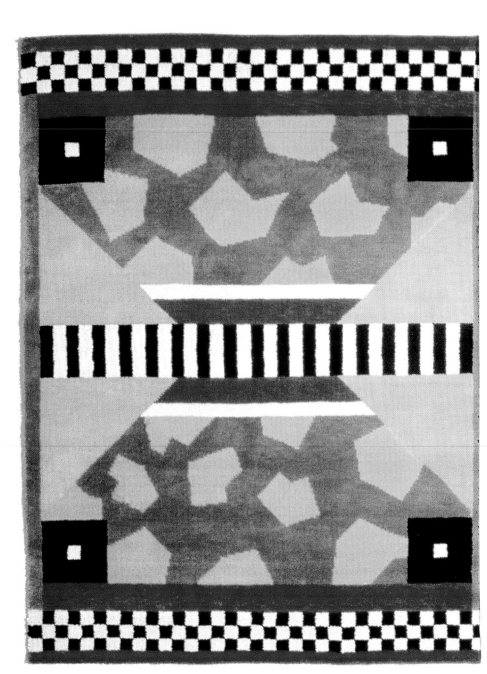

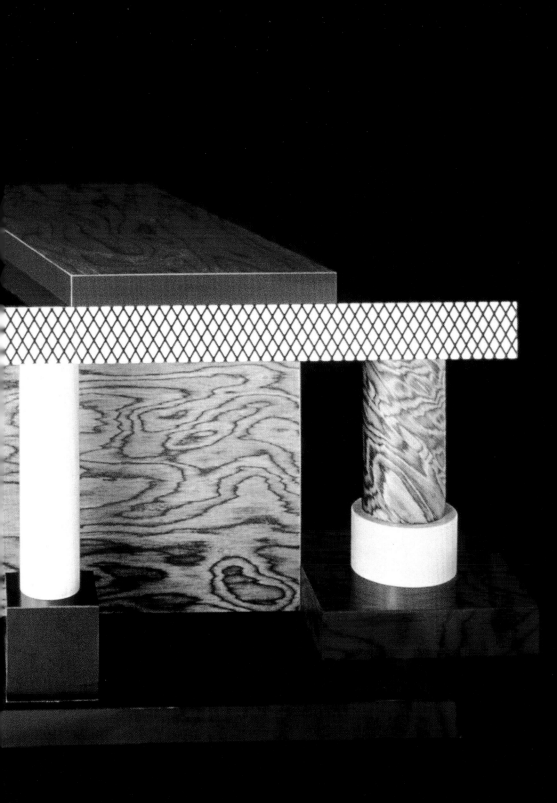

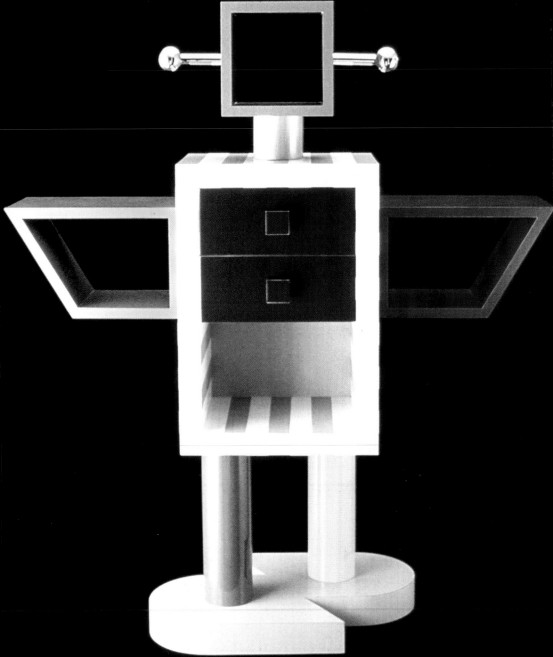

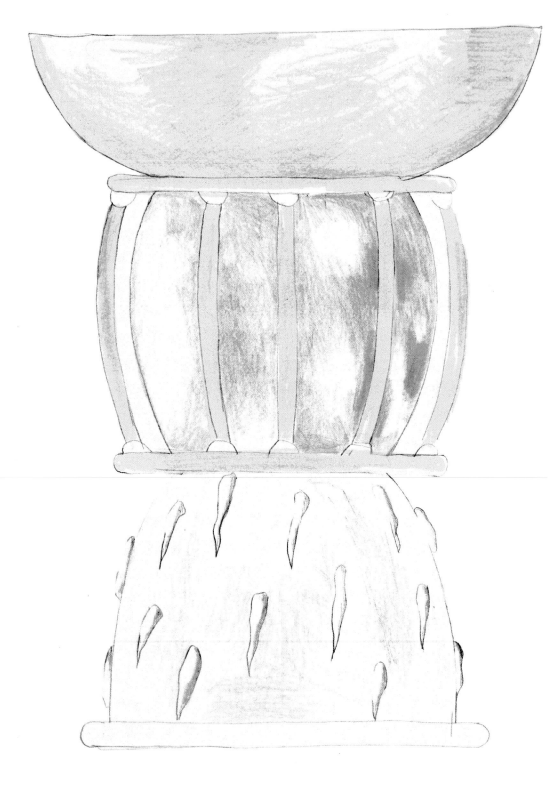

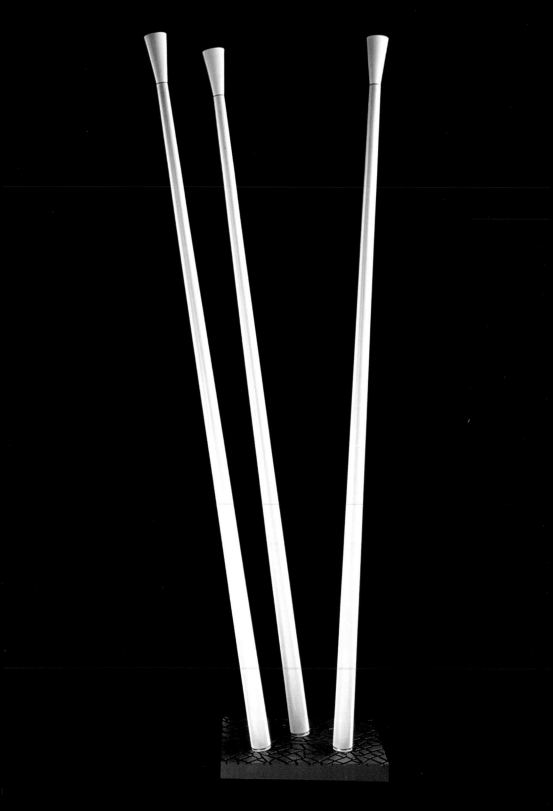

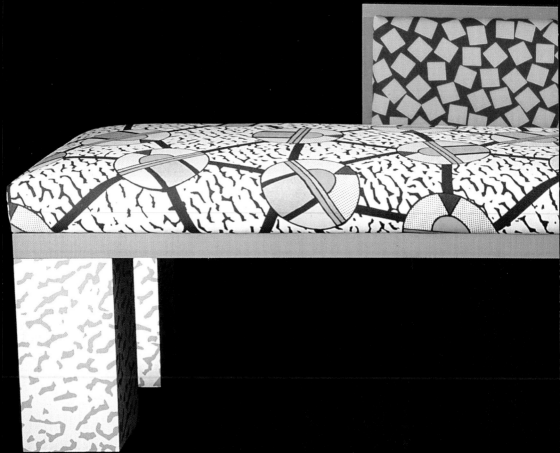

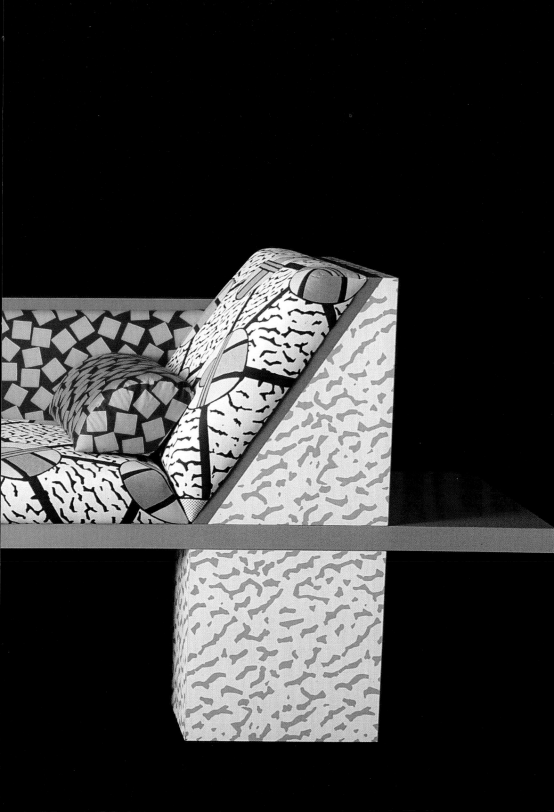

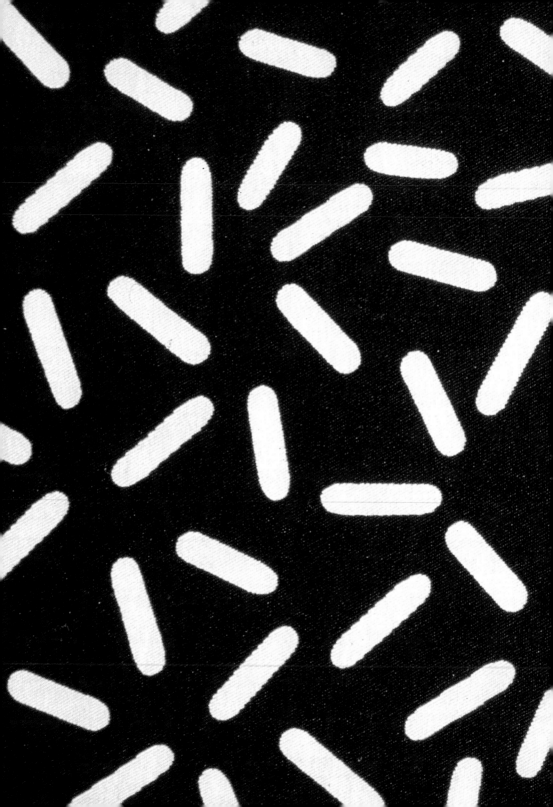

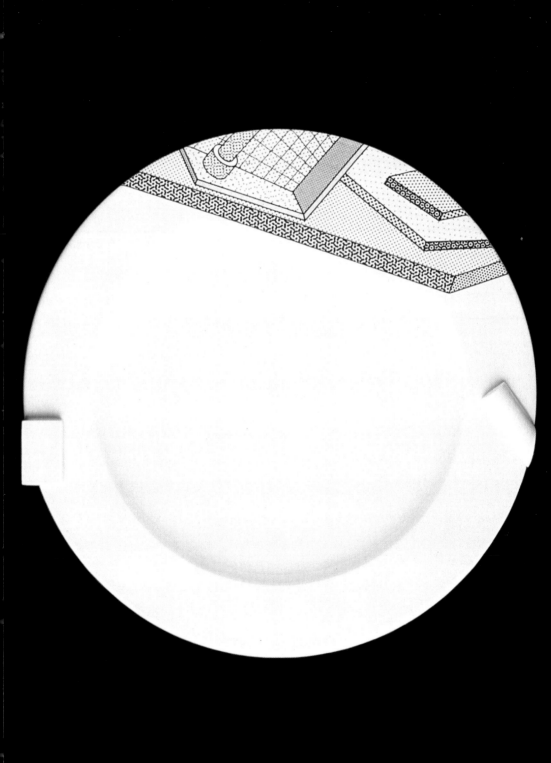

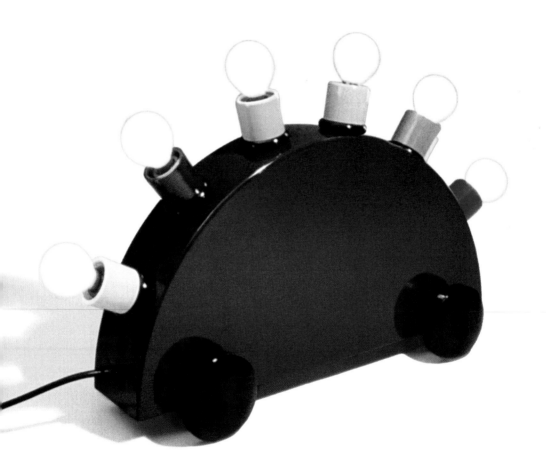

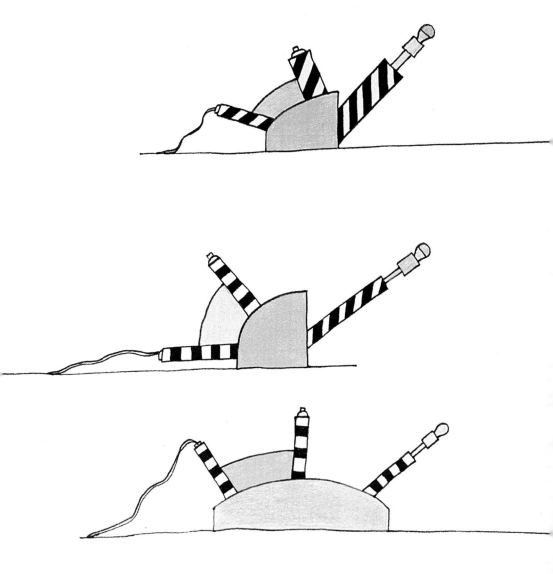

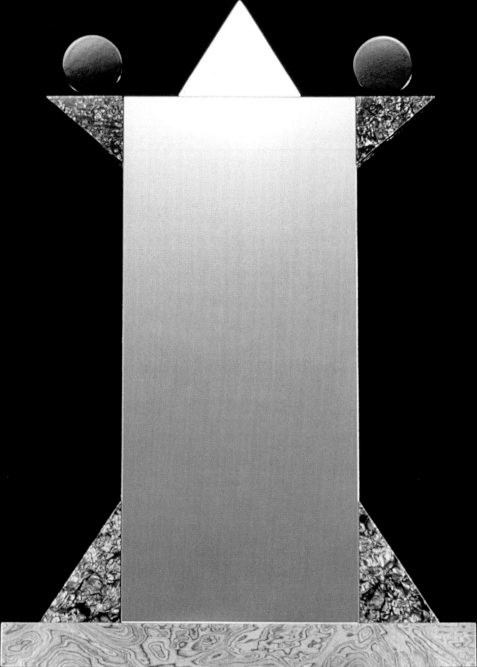

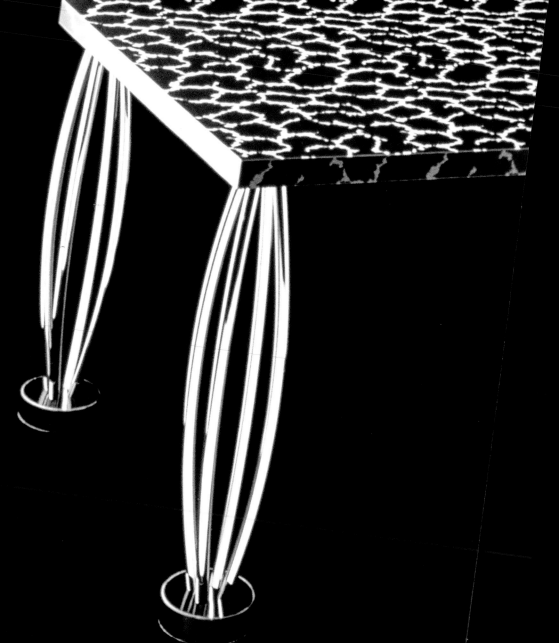

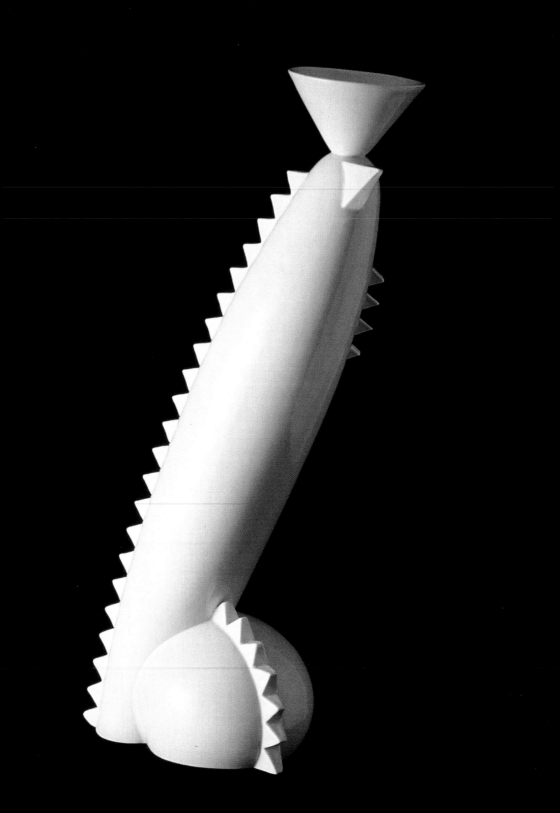

Chronology

1980   On 11 December, the famous Italian designer Ettore Sottsass, who graduated in architecture from the Turin Polytechnic in 1939, sets up Memphis with a group of young designers, among them Marco Zanini, Aldo Cibic, Matteo Thun, Michele De Lucchi, Martine Bedin, Nathalie Du Pasquier and George James Sowden. Their aim is to invent a 'new design' which will be challenging and witty.

1981   In February the Memphis project takes shape in the form of one hundred drawings – designs for a new kind of furniture and artefacts which are brightly coloured, asymmetrical in shape and have a surface decoration.
In June Sottsass finds financial backers and the Memphis company is formed. It consists of five partners: Ernesto Gismondi, chairman of Artemide, Fausto Celati, another manufacturer, Renzo Brugola, cabinet-maker and a friend of Sottsass, and Brunella and Mario Godani, the owners of the showroom *Arc 74* in Milan (and later of the *Design Gallery*). Gismondi, the principal shareholder, is responsible for the commercial production and distribution of the Memphis Milano collections on the international market.
On 18 September, at the same time as the Milan Salon furniture show, Memphis' first collection is launched at the *Arc 74* showroom. It consists of fifty-five designs, with thirty pieces of furniture, three clocks, eleven lamps and eleven ceramic pieces. Some of them are the work of foreign makers – Javier Mariscal, Michael Graves, Peter Shire, Shiro Kuramata and Hans Hollein.

1982   In September Memphis' second collection is shown at the *Design Gallery* in Milan.
The dress designer Karl Lagerfeld buys the first two collections to furnish his apartment in Monte Carlo.

1983   Third collection. The chair called *First*, by Michele De Lucchi, is the most commercially successful of Memphis' designs. It is still in production and to date five thousand have been sold.

1984   Fourth collection.

1985   Fifth collection.

1986   Sixth collection.

1987   Seventh collection. Some of the work shown is designed by the young Milanese designers Massimo Iosa Ghini, Beppe Caturegli, Angelo Micheli, Ferruccio Laviani and Marco Zanuso Jr.

Mizar vase, Ettore Sottsass, blue transparent glass with multi-coloured handles (diam. 30 cm, height 32 cm), Memphis Milano 1982. © Memphis, Milan.

| 1988 | A new group of lamps called 'Luci-Lights' is shown in Memphis' last collection. End of the movement: the group gathered together by Ettore Sottsass disperses. |

1988   A new group of lamps called 'Luci-Lights' is shown in Memphis' last collection. End of the movement: the group gathered together by Ettore Sottsass disperses.

1989   Several retrospectives are held in museums all over the world, while the three hundred Memphis Milano pieces designed over eight years continue to be available on the international market.
New collections are produced for the Memphis Srl company, which is independent from the famous original group: 'Meta-Memphis' (1989–1991), later 'Meta'; 'Memphis Extra' (1992, 1993 and 1994), later 'Extra'; and 'Easy Home by Alessandro Mendini' (1995).

1996   The Memphis company is bought by its managing director Alberto Bianchi Albrici from Ernesto Gismondi, the original owner. The individual, small-scale production of Memphis Milano classics continues.

1997   Albrici opens his gallery, *Post-Design*, in Milan, where he shows and sells Memphis Srl's various products. He also shows new work with the *Post-Design* trademark.

Bibliography

Anargyros, Sophie, *Le Style des années quatre vingt, architecture, décoration, design*, Paris, 1986

Atsushi, Sato, *Sottsass, 151 Drawings*, Tokyo, 1997

Bischofberger, Bruno (ed.), *Ettore Sottsass, Ceramics*, London and New York, 1995

Branzi, Andrea, *The Hot House: Italian New Wave Design*, London and New York, 1984

Bure, Gilles de, *Ettore Sottsass Jr*, Paris, 1987

Casciani, Stefano, and Di Pietrantonio, Giacinto, *Design in Italia, 1950–1990*, Milan, 1991

Dormer, Peter, *Design Since 1945*, London and New York, 1993

Fitoussi, Brigitte, *Objets affectifs, Le Nouveau design de la table*, Paris, 1993

Guidot, Raymond, *Histoire du design, 1940–1990*, Paris, 1994

Radice, Barbara, *Ettore Sottsass, A Critical Biography*, London and New York, 1993

Radice, Barbara, *Memphis, Research, Experiences, Results, Failures and Successes of New Design*, London and New York, 1987

Radice, Barbara, *Memphis, The New International Style*, Milan, 1981

Sambonet, Guia, *Alchimia, 1977–1987*, Turin, 1987

Sambonet, Guia, *Ettore Sottsass, Mobili e qualche arredamento*, Milan, 1985

Sottsass, Ettore, *The Curious Mr Sottsass, Photographing Design and Desire*, London and New York, 1996

Ettore Sottsass, Paris, 1994

Ettore Sottsass, La darrera Oportunitat d'esser Avant Guarda, Barcelona, 1993

Sparke, Penny, *Italian Design, 1870 to the Present*, London, 1988

Venturi, Robert, *De l'ambiguïté en architecture*, Paris, 1976 (1st edn, Museum of Modern Art, New York, 1966)

Ashoka *lamp, Ettore Sottsass, painted metal (light bulbs: 1 x 50 W, 5 x 40W, 12 V–E 14), Memphis Milano 1981. © Memphis, Milan.*

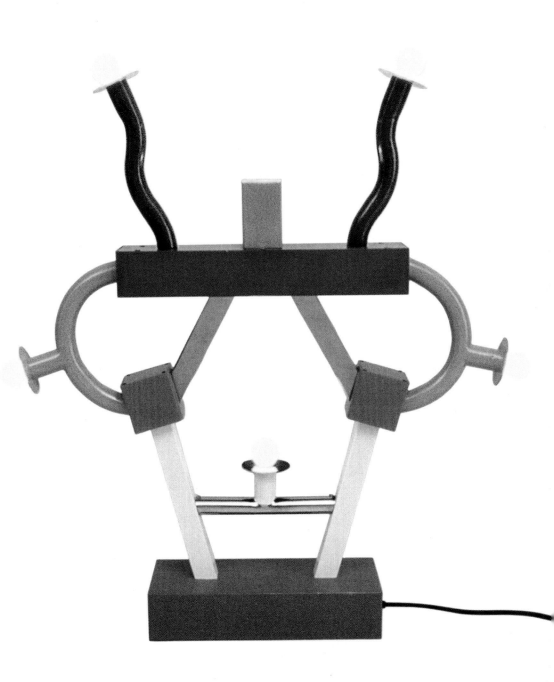

Memphis

Memphis group portrait, October 1982. From left to right: foreground, Michele De Lucchi, Marco Zanini; second row, Barbara Radice, Aldo Cibic, Ettore Sottsass, Ernesto Gismondi, George James Sowden; third row, Nathalie Du Pasquier, Jerry Taylor, Martine Bedin, Matteo Thun, Christoph Radl, Egidio di Rosa. © Barbara Radice, Milan. **Invitation for the first Memphis exhibition in Milan,** September 1981. © Barbara Radice, Milan.

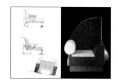

Lido **sofa,** Michele De Lucchi, 1982, coloured sketches on paper. © Studio De Lucchi, Milan.
Bel Air **armchair,** Peter Shire, wooden frame with wool or cotton covering (115 x 110 x 125 cm), Memphis Milano 1982. © Memphis, Milan.

Flamingo **bedside table,** Michele De Lucchi, laminated plastic and lacquered wood (35 x 50 x 90 cm), Memphis Milano 1984. © Nestor Perkal/Gobelin, Paris.
Hilton **trolley,** Javier Mariscal, metal and glass (125 x 45 x 85 cm), Memphis Milano 1981. © Memphis, Milan.

Sirio **vase,** Ettore Sottsass, blown glass (height 35 cm), Memphis Milano 1982. © Memphis, Milan.
Rigel, spherical vessel with lid and narrow stem, transparent blue, black, green and red glass (height 35 cm), Memphis Milano 1982. © Memphis, Milan.

Ettore Sottsass with examples of his work, 1976. © Keystone, Paris.

Tigris **vase,** Ettore Sottsass, porcelain (diam. 19 cm, height 39 cm), Memphis Milano 1983. © Memphis, Milan.
Euphrates **vase,** Ettore Sottsass, porcelain (diam. 22 cm, height 40 cm), Memphis Milano 1983. © Memphis, Milan.

Murmansk **fruit basket,** Ettore Sottsass, silver (diam. 35 cm, height 30 cm), Memphis Milano 1982. © Memphis, Milan.
Colorado **teapot,** Marco Zanini, ceramic (29 x 23 cm), Memphis Milano 1983. © Memphis, Milan.

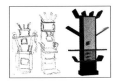

Sketches for the *Factotum* **furniture series,** Ettore Sottsass, 1980, coloured pencil on paper. © Ettore Sottsass, Milan.
Casablanca **buffet,** Ettore Sottsass, laminated plastic with drawers and cupboard (151 x 42 x 230 cm, depth 32 cm), Memphis Milano 1981. © Memphis, Milan.

Brazil **console table,** Peter Shire, lacquered wood (205 x 80 x 72 cm), Memphis Milano 1981. © Memphis, Milan.

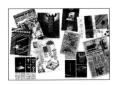

Newspaper cuttings on Memphis from all over the world. © Barbara Radice/ Ettore Sottsass.

Memphis furniture in a room setting. *Super* lamp by Martine Bedin, *First* chair by Michele De Lucchi, *Vitrine d'Antibes* by George James Sowden, *Sirio* vase by Ettore Sottsass. © Nestor Perkal, Paris/Didier Cazabon.
Kristall **pedestal table,** Michele De Lucchi, laminated plastic, wood and metal (50 x 67 x 62 cm), Memphis Milano 1981. © Memphis, Milan.

The *Esprit* **shop** in Cologne, designed 1985–1986 by the Sottsass Associati practice. In the foreground, Michele De Lucchi's *First* chair, wood and metal (59 x 50 x 90 cm), Memphis Milano 1983. © Photo: Tom Vack, Blevio.

Tawaraya **ring,** Masanori Umeda, Memphis Milano 1981. © Sotheby's, London.

Cleopatra **pedestal table,** Marco Zanuso Jr, turned wood and metal (diam. 35 cm, height 72 cm), Memphis Milano 1987. © Memphis, Milan.
Juliette **chair,** Massimo Iosa-Ghini, metal, plastic and straw (54 x 77 x 90 cm). Memphis Milano 1987. © Memphis, Milan.

Chi a paura del manierismo ('who's afraid of mannerism'), Ettore Sottsass, 1986, pencil on paper (28 x 35 cm). © Ettore Sottsass, Milan.
Nonsense Architettonico ('architectural nonsense'), Ettore Sottsass, 1976, tempera on paper (34 x 46 cm). © Ettore Sottsass, Milan.

Arizona **carpet,** Nathalie Du Pasquier, handwoven wool (250 x 180 cm), Memphis Milano 1983. © Nestor Perkal, Paris.
Chair, George James Sowden, 1985, lacquered wood and laminated plastic. Nestor Perkal Collection. © Memphis, Milan.

Tartar **console table,** Ettore Sottsass, imitation wood grain on laminated plastic (195 x 85 x 78 cm), Memphis Milano 1985. © Memphis, Milan.

Ginza, Masanori Umeda, 'robot' piece of furniture with drawers and shelves, laminated plastic and wood (55 x 42 x 175 cm), Memphis Milano 1982. © Nestor Perkal/Studio Azzurro.
Furniture displayed in the *Nestor Perkal* **boutique** in Paris. Chair by Marco Zanini, cabinet by Matteo Thun, lamp, tall pedestal table and ceramic by Ettore Sottsass. © Nestor Perkal/Didier Cazabon, Paris.

Glass vessel, Ettore Sottsass, 1983, pencil on paper (30 x 46 cm). © Ettore Sottsass, Milan.
Alcor **vase,** Ettore Sottsass, blown glass (height 48 cm), Memphis Milano 1983. © Memphis, Milan.

Buenos Aires **standard lamp,** Aldo Cibic and Cesare Ongaro, adjustable stands, porcelain diffusers, 150 W halogen light bulbs (52 x 39 x 220 cm), Memphis Milano 1986. © Memphis, Milan.
Magnolia **bookshelf,** Andrea Branzi, metal, laminated plastic and glass, with plastic palm trees (200 x 50 x 208 cm), Memphis Milano 1985. © Memphis, Milan.

Royal **sofa,** Nathalie Du Pasquier, laminated plastic and cotton fabric, fabric design for cushion and armrest by George James Sowden (220 x 75 x 95 cm), Memphis Milano 1983. © Memphis, Milan.

Barbaric Furniture, Ettore Sottsass, 1985, watercolour on paper. © Ettore Sottsass, Milan.
Kyoto **table,** Shiro Kuramata, metal, terrazzo and glass (diam. 60 cm, height 70 cm), Memphis Milano 1983. © Memphis, Milan.

Letraset **fabric,** Ettore Sottsass, cotton (height 140 cm), Memphis Milano 1983. © Memphis, Milan.
Lettuce **plate,** Ettore Sottsass, decorated white ceramic (diam. 30 cm), Memphis Milano 1985. © Memphis, Milan.

Super **lamp,** Martine Bedin, fibreglass and rubber, E 14, 40 W light bulbs (height 30 cm), Memphis Milano 1981.© Memphis, Milan.
Sketch designs for a metal lamp, Michele De Lucchi, 1980. © Studio De Lucchi, Milan.

Tahiti **lamp,** Ettore Sottsass, laminated plastic and metal, 50 W, 12 V halogen light bulbs (height 60 cm), Memphis Milano 1981. © Memphis, Milan.
Diva **mirror,** Ettore Sottsass, laminated plastic (76 x 5 x 108 cm), Memphis Milano 1984. © Memphis, Milan.

City **table,** Ettore Sottsass, laminated plastic and metal (160 x 85 x 72 cm), Memphis Milano 1983. © Memphis, Milan.

Volga **'Soliflore' vase,** Matteo Thun, porcelain (diam. 15 cm), Memphis Milano 1983. © Memphis, Milan.
Carrot **vase,** Nathalie Du Pasquier, ceramic (height 30 cm), Memphis Milano 1985. © Memphis, Milan.

Acknowledgments

The author and publishers would like to thank Ettore Sottsass, Barbara Radice, Michele De Lucchi, Alberto Bianchi Albrici and Elena Princiroli (Memphis Srl), Monica del Torchio (Studio De Lucchi), Manuella (Sottsass Ass.), Nestor Perkal, Roger von Bary, Philippe Garner (Sotheby's), Christine Sorin (Centre Georges Pompidou), Catherine Seignouret (Keystone), Tom Vack, Arnaud Maillard and Martine Bedin.